EISENHOWER PUBLIC LIBRARY

3 1134 00414 7062

W9-AUY-082

2/15

Eisenhower Public Library
4613 N. Oketo Avenue
Harwood Heights, IL 60706
708-867-7828

Published in 2015 by The Rosen Publishing Group, Inc.
29 East 21st Street, New York, NY 10010

Copyright © 2015 Weldon Owen Pty Ltd. Originally published in 2011 by Discovery Communications, LLC

Original copyright © 2011 Discovery Communications, LLC. Discovery Education™ and the Discovery Education logo are trademarks of Discovery Communications, LLC, used under license. All rights reserved.

All rights reserved. No part of this book may be reproduced in any form without permission in writing from the publisher, except by a reviewer.

Photo Credits: **KEY** tl=top left; bl=bottom left; bc=bottom center; bg=background

CiS = istockphoto.com; PECD = PhotoEssentials; NHPA = NHPA/Photoshot

**6**bc iS; **11**tl PECD; **12**bl iS; **16**bl iS; **19**bc NHPA; **20**bc iS; **24**bc iS; **30**bg PDCD

All illustrations copyright Weldon Owen Pty Ltd

WELDON OWEN PTY LTD
Managing Director:  Kay Scarlett
Creative Director:  Sue Burk
Publisher:  Helen Bateman
Senior Vice: President, International Sales:  Stuart Laurence
Vice President Sales North America:  Ellen Towell
Administration Manager, International Sales:  Kristine Ravn

Library of Congress Cataloging-in-Publication Data

Costain, Meredith, author.
 Reptiles : cold-blooded creatures by Meredith Costain.
     pages cm. — (Discovery education. Animals)
 Includes index.
 ISBN 978-1-4777-6936-2 (library binding) — ISBN 978-1-4777-6937-9 (pbk.) —
ISBN 978-1-4777-6938-6 (6-pack)
 1. Reptiles—Juvenile literature. 2. Reptiles—Physiology—Juvenile literature. I. Title.
 QL644.2.C65 2015
 597.9—dc23
                                        2013047551

Manufactured in the United States of America

CPSIA Compliance Information: Batch #WS14PK3: For Further Information contact Rosen Publishing, New York, New York at 1-800-237-9932

**ANIMALS**

# REPTILES
## COLD-BLOODED CREATURES

Meredith Costain

**PowerKiDS** press

New York

# Contents

# What Is a Reptile?

Reptiles are a type of vertebrate, or animal with a backbone. Their bodies are covered in tough scales or shells. Reptiles come in many different shapes and sizes, from the tiny dwarf gecko to the saltwater crocodile. They live in many different habitats, from oceans to deserts, and are found on every continent of the world except Antarctica.

**Crocodilian**
There are 23 different species of crocodilians, including crocodiles, alligators, gharials, and caimans.

## MEET THE ANCESTORS

By studying fossils, scientists are able to find out what the ancestors of current-day reptiles looked like. The earliest relatives of reptiles were amphibians.

**First reptiles**
The first reptiles lived 315 million years ago and were 8 inches (20 cm) long.

**First lizards**
The first lizards looked like modern geckos. They lived around 150 million years ago.

**First crocodiles**
With strong jaws and powerful tails, the first crocodiles lived 145 million years ago.

**First turtles**
Turtles that lived 210 million years ago looked similar to the turtles of today, with heavily armored shells.

Tortoise

Turtle

## Tortoise and turtle
The Testudine group of reptiles is made up of turtles and tortoises. There are around 300 different species.

## Tuatara
The tuatara is the oldest living relative of snakes and lizards. It is found only in New Zealand.

## Lizard
There are more than 5,000 different species of lizards. Unlike snakes, lizards have limbs, eyelids, and external ears.

## Snake
About 3,400 different types of snakes exist. Most are non-venomous. Some swallow their prey alive.

# Controlling Body Heat

**Color change**
The warmth of the Sun changes the red-headed agama's skin from brown to bright red and blue.

Although reptiles are described as being "cold-blooded," they can be as warm as birds or mammals when they are moving. Instead of creating their own body heat, reptiles depend on the Sun and warm surfaces to heat their bodies. They move to a warm place to raise their body temperature, and to a cooler place to lower it.

## KEEPING COOL

Reptiles cool themselves down by heading out of the Sun into the shade, or by taking a dip in a pool of water.

**Fancy footwork**
Fringe-toed lizards hop from one foot to the other when they are walking across hot sand.

**Gaping jaws**
Black caimans hold their jaws open to help cool the blood in their thick tongue.

**Skin shedders**
Snakes shed their outer skin layer in one piece, starting at the lips.

# Scales or Shells

Reptiles have tough, dry skin. The skin has a thick layer of keratin, a substance that makes up fingernails, hooves, and horns. Lizards and snakes have scales. Crocodiles and alligators have bony plates beneath their skin. Every now and then, reptiles shed their outer skin layer. Turtles and tortoises have bony shells. The shell's inner layer is made up of about 60 bones.

## SHELL ANATOMY

The outer layer of a turtle shell is covered by horny scales called scutes. The backbone and ribs are joined to the upper shell.

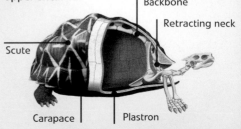

Backbone

Retracting neck

Scute

Carapace

Plastron

## Egg care

Some pythons coil themselves around their eggs and vibrate their body to help keep the eggs warm. This also protects the eggs from predators.

### Fact or Fiction?

In folktales, female sea turtles are said to "cry" when they leave the ocean to lay their eggs. What they are really doing, however, is getting rid of excess salt.

# Egg Layers

Female crocodilians care for their eggs and newly hatched young. They build nests for the eggs, scraping soil and plants into mounds, or burying them in sand. The mothers guard their nests, scaring away predators. They stay with their young until they are ready to look after themselves. Turtles scoop deep holes in sand, laying up to 100 eggs at a time. Snakes do not look after their young once they have hatched.

## Gentle jaws

Female alligators gently carry their newly hatched babies to a safe place in their sharp-toothed jaws.

## RACE TO THE SEA

Once they hatch from their shells, newborn flatback turtles race to the sea. They travel in a group to help protect themselves from predators, such as birds and crabs. Sharks and other fish wait for them in the ocean. Usually only 1 turtle in 100 will survive.

# What Is a Crocodilian?

There are 23 different crocodilian species, including two kinds of alligators, 13 crocodiles, six caimans, and two gharials. Apart from the Chinese alligator, crocodilians live where the weather is warm. At 20 feet (6 m) long, the saltwater crocodile is the largest species. Cuvier's dwarf caiman, at 5 feet (1.5 m), is the smallest. Crocodilians stay close to water, hunting for insects, frogs, fish, turtles, and birds.

## GHARIAL

The gharial lives in large rivers in Asia. It is less fierce than a crocodile and alligator, with weaker legs. It hunts fish, striking swiftly with its narrow snout as the fish swim past.

## Bubble makers

When male American alligators rumble, the vibrations shoot water bubbles up to 2 feet (60 cm) above the surface. The deep rumblings are so powerful they can be sensed by female alligators 1 mile (1.6 km) away.

## Deep Freeze

Chinese and American alligators live in areas that become so cold in winter, ice forms on the surface of ponds and streams. The alligators find a shallow pool and lie in the warmer water below the ice, with only their nose above the surface.

## That's Amazing!

Crocodilians make a great deal of noise to attract a mate or warn off rivals. They roar and rumble, slap their head around, or snort air through their nostrils.

# Crocodilian Behavior

Crocodilians are some of the world's largest and most dangerous reptiles. The Nile crocodile's jaws are strong enough to shatter bones, and they are able to swallow small prey whole. Many crocodilian species are able to control their body temperature through their behavior. Nile crocodiles lie basking in the Sun on riverbanks during the day. But at nightfall, when the air temperature drops, they move down into the warmer water.

**Sneak attack**
Crocodilians sneak up on their prey. They lie low in the water, with only their eyes, ears, and nostrils above the surface. They glide silently toward their victim, then pounce on it.

**Floaters**
Crocodilians float easily. This allows them to save their energy for attacks.

## Death roll

Nile crocodiles drag their prey into water to kill it. They twist and turn, thrashing their victims against the water until they are too confused to escape.

## UNDERWATER ADAPTATION

Crocodilians have external nostrils at the tip of their jaws. This lets them breathe when the rest of their body is underwater. Their internal nostrils are farther along at the back of the throat. A throat flap stops water from coming into the windpipe when they are thrashing underwater, struggling with prey.

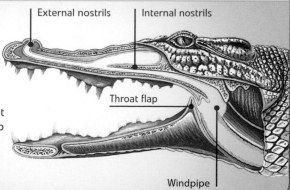

External nostrils

Internal nostrils

Throat flap

Windpipe

# What Is a Lizard?

L izards are found on all continents except Antarctica. There are more than 5,000 different kinds. The major groups of lizards include geckos, skinks, chameleons, iguanas, and Gila monsters. Lizards eat mainly insects, and sometimes plants. Large lizards eat other reptiles, as well as small mammals and birds. All lizards have scales to prevent them from drying out when it is hot.

## CLAWS AND TOES

The shape of a lizard's foot is linked to the way it moves. Runners have long toes, while swimmers' toes are webbed. Climbers have needle-sharp claws or sticky pads.

**Claspers**
Chameleons have two groups of toes that allow them to grasp narrow branches tightly.

**Diggers**
Monitor lizards have thick, sharp claws to dig hard soil and attack prey.

**Sand-dwellers**
Desert geckos have webbed feet, which help them to move across sand dunes.

**Runners**
The long toes of the whiptail lizard increase its stride, helping it to run fast.

## After dark

The tokay gecko hunts at night. It stalks its prey slowly at first, then snatches it up with one quick movement.

**Suction cups**
The pads beneath a gecko's toes are covered with millions of tiny hairs. These act like sticky suction cups.

*Tokay geckos are able to cling to walls and walk upside down.*

# Escape Methods

Because lizards have many predators, they have developed several clever ways to protect themselves. Chameleons can change color, which often helps them to blend in with their background. They stay completely still if a predator comes near. Some lizards surprise their attacker by hissing or sticking out their tongues, giving themselves a chance to escape. Others simply outrun them, or dive into water where they cannot be followed. The armadillo girdle-tailed lizard curls itself into a ball, protecting itself with a prickly set of spines.

**Frilled lizard**
The Australian frilled lizard opens its mouth wide, hisses, and puffs out its neck frills to scare away predators.

**Blood spurt**
Special muscles squirt a smelly stream of blood from the lizard's eyes.

**Horns and scales**
Bony head horns and spiny scales make the lizard difficult to swallow.

**Regal horned lizard**
Its small size should make the regal horned lizard easy prey. However, it has several unique ways to stay safe.

**Frills**
The extended neck frills make the lizard look bigger than it actually is.

## ESCAPE PLAN

Most lizards drop all or part of their tail if a predator grabs it. Only a small amount of blood is lost. A new tail, which may be plain in color, soon grows from the stump.

# What Is a Snake?

There are about 3,400 species of snakes in the world. Of these, less than a quarter are venomous, and they will strike only if threatened. Snakes have wide jaws that allow them to swallow their prey whole. Constrictors wrap their bodies tightly around their prey to suffocate it first.

**Lungs**
Most snakes have only one working lung, which is long and narrow.

**Small intestine**
The long, tubular small intestine absorbs nutrients from the stomach.

**Stomach**
The stomach has elastic, expandable walls and strong digestive juices.

**Ribs**
The backbone has between 150 and 450 vertebrae, each with two ribs.

## FANGS

Venomous snakes kill their prey by injecting them with poison with their fangs. There are several types of fangs.

**At the ready**
Short, hollow, front fangs are always ready to strike.

**In the rear**
Fangs with grooves for venom flow are set at the back of a snake's jaw.

**Foldaway**
Long fangs can be folded away into the mouth, then unfolded when needed.

## Jacobson's organ

Snakes stick out their tongue to collect information for their Jacobson's organ, located in the roof of their mouth. This organ helps them decide if another snake is a possible mate or rival.

Jacobson's organ

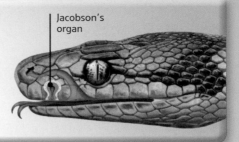

## Strike out

The highly toxic venom of the viper snake makes it one of the deadliest snakes in the world.

**Venom gland**
Liquid venom is stored in a gland before moving through venom ducts to the fangs.

**Eyes**
Eyes are covered with a clear, see-through, non-moving scale.

**Forked tongue**
The tongue passes information about smell back to the brain.

**Fangs**
The long fangs are hinged, ready to spring into action.

## Scales

A snake's scales provide clues about where it lives. Wetland snakes have keeled scales. Burrowers have smooth ones. Sea snakes have rough, granular scales.

Keeled scales

Smooth scales

Granular scales

**Eyes**
The size of a snake's eyes relates to whether it hunts at night (small) or during the day (big).

Small eyes

Big eyes

# Snake Behavior

All snakes eat animals. They have different ways of catching and killing them. Some snakes ambush, stalk, or chase after their prey. Others choose "easy" prey, such as bird or reptile eggs. Pythons and boa constrictors coil themselves around their prey and squeeze it until it suffocates. Venomous snakes, such as the king cobra, inject their prey with poison.

**Heat sensors**
A rattlesnake's heat-sensing organs are so accurate that it can strike even when it is totally dark.

## HOW SNAKES MOVE

Snakes have developed different ways to move around. The method they use depends on how big they are, how fast they want to travel, and whether the surface is smooth or rough.

**Sidewinder**
Desert vipers throw coils of their body sideways to move across loose sand.

**S-shaped waves**
Muscles send S-shaped waves along the body from front to back.

**Caterpillar-style**
Heavy snakes, such as pythons, ripple their bellies to inch forward like a caterpillar.

**Concertina-style**
The snake bends its body like an accordion, then straightens itself out to move forward.

**Change of color**
Green tree pythons are bright yellow or brown when
they hatch. They take up to three years to turn green.

## All in one

Pythons swallow their prey whole.
They slowly "walk" their jaws
forward until they are wide enough
to take in large animals, which can
take months to digest.

# Tortoises and Turtles

The oldest kinds of reptiles are tortoises and turtles. They both have a bony shell built into their skeleton. There are 310 different species, spread over most parts of the world. Turtles live mainly in or near freshwater, while more than 50 tortoise species live on land.

**Cleaning crew**
Cleaner wrasse are small fish that clean barnacles from sea turtles' shells.

## MOBILE HOMES

Land turtles have thick heavy shells, which they rely on for defense. The light, smooth shells of aquatic turtles improve their swimming speed.

**Slider turtle**
The thin, streamlined shell of the slider helps it to swim efficiently.

**Sea turtle**
The lightweight shells of sea turtles are not large enough to hide their arms and legs.

**Radiated tortoise**
Heavy, domed shells offer protection from predators, but slow tortoises down.

**Box turtle**
Box turtles pull their head and legs inside their domed shells for protection against predators.

## Hawksbill turtle

The hawksbill turtle is a sea turtle. Its shell is thinner and lighter than a land turtle's, and it has flippers for swimming.

**Bony paddle**
The flipper's thick arm bones and long fingers help turtles power through water.

# Tortoise and Turtle Behavior

**M**ost land tortoises live in dry environments or deserts. Their heavy shells offer protection from predators, but slow down their movements to a speed of about 295 feet (90 m) an hour. Freshwater turtles ambush their prey, insects and fish, underwater. Semiterrestrial turtles hunt on land as well as in the water. Some hibernate underwater in mud, while others find burrows on land.

*That's Amazing!*
Musk turtles give off a nasty smell if they are picked up by predators. Their scientific name has the same meaning as their nickname—stinkpot!

## KEEPING COOL

Tortoises in warm areas move around only in the morning or late afternoon. During the hottest part of the day, they lie under a shady tree or burrow into soil. The gopher tortoise spends most of its time in a burrow, sheltering from both summer heat and winter cold.

**Snapping turtle**
The alligator snapping turtle lures fish into its powerful jaws by waving its wormlike tongue. Its jaws are strong enough to bite off your finger.

**Water collectors**
Giant saddleback tortoises collect water from cactus plants if there has been no rain. Once the rain arrives, they gather around puddles and drink as much as they can.

# Reptile Fact File

At 1,500 pounds (680 kg), the leatherback turtle is the heaviest reptile. The smallest and lightest is the tiny 0.6-inch (16-mm) Jaragua Sphaero, or dwarf gecko. Sea turtles, which swim 18 miles (29 km) a day, are the fastest reptiles and Galápagos tortoises, which swim 4 miles (6.4 km) a day, are the slowest.

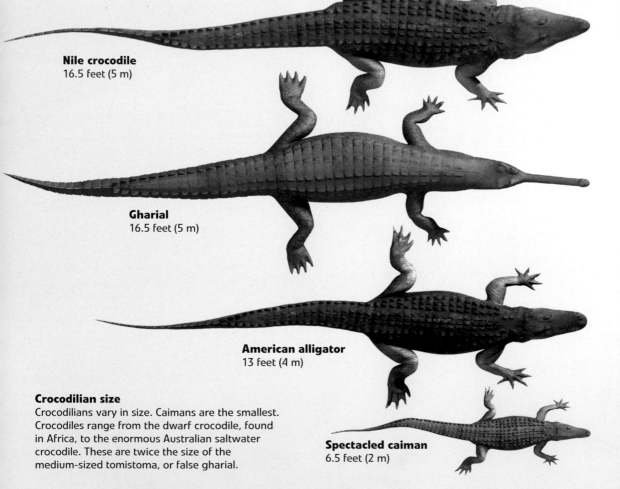

**Nile crocodile**
16.5 feet (5 m)

**Gharial**
16.5 feet (5 m)

**American alligator**
13 feet (4 m)

**Crocodilian size**
Crocodilians vary in size. Caimans are the smallest. Crocodiles range from the dwarf crocodile, found in Africa, to the enormous Australian saltwater crocodile. These are twice the size of the medium-sized tomistoma, or false gharial.

**Spectacled caiman**
6.5 feet (2 m)

**Anaconda**
33 feet (10 m)

**Snake poison**
The biggest snakes are not always the most dangerous. The venom of the yellow-bellied sea snake is strong enough to kill much larger prey within minutes.

**Boa constrictor**
14.5 feet (4.5 m)

**Rattlesnake**
7 feet (2.2 m)

**Madagascan spider tortoise**
4 inches (10 cm)

**Yellow-bellied sea snake**
2.5 feet (0.8 m)

**South American tortoise**
8 inches (20 cm)

**Tortoises**
The tiny Madagascan spider tortoise could easily sit on the back of a South American tortoise, which could rest on the back of the wheelbarrow-sized tortoise from the Galápagos islands.

**Galápagos tortoise**
59 inches (1.5 m)

**Pygmy chameleon**
1.5 inches (3.5 cm)

**Lizard size**
Lizards range in size from the tiny Jaragua Sphaero, which is small enough to fit on a coin, to the giant Komodo dragon, which can weigh more than 120 pounds (55 kg).

**Madagascar day gecko**
9 inches (22 cm)

**Scaly-foot**
18 inches (45 cm)

**Green iguana**
6.5 feet (2 m)

**Komodo dragon**
10 feet (3 m)

# Over to You

Research the following records to create a Reptile Hall of Fame. Some of the information can be found in this book.

 **1** Largest reptile

 **2** Smallest reptile

 **3** Heaviest reptile

 **4** Longest reptile

 **5** Fastest reptile in water

 **6** Fastest reptile on land

 **7** Slowest reptile

 **8** Reptile with the stickiest feet

 **9** Most venomous reptile

 **10** Smelliest reptile

**Answers: 1** Saltwater crocodile **2** Jaragua Sphaero (also known as dwarf gecko) **3** Leatherback turtle **4** Anaconda **5** Pacific leatherback turtle **6** Black mamba snake **7** Giant tortoise from the Galapagos Islands **8** Gecko **9** Inland taipan **10** Musk turtle (nicknamed "stinkpot")

# Glossary

**adaptation**
(a-dap-TAY-shun) The way animal species change to suit their environment.

**ambush**
(AM-bush) To hide, keep very still, then pounce on the surprised prey.

**amphibians**
(am-FIH-bee-unz) Animals with moist skin that lay their eggs in water. They usually begin life in the water as tadpoles with gills, and later develop lungs.

**ancestor** (AN-ses-ter)
A plant or animal from which a later form evolved.

**basking**
(BASK-ing) Stretching out in the warm sunshine.

**carapace**
(KER-uh-pays) The upper or back part of a turtle's or tortoise's shell.

**cold–blooded**
(KOHLD-bluh-did) Unable to keep its body at the same temperature by internal means.

**crocodilian**
(krah-kuh-DIL-yun) A member of the order Crocodilia, which includes crocodiles, caimans, alligators, gharials, and tomistomas.

**digest** (dy-JEST) To break down food so it can be absorbed into the body.

**external** (ek-STER-nul) On the outside.

**flippers** (FLIH-perz) The broad front legs of sea turtles that act like paddles to move them through water.

**granular** (GRAN-yuh-lur) Having a grainy texture.

**habitat** (HA-buh-tat) The place where an animal naturally lives.

**internal** (in-TUR-nel) On the inside.

**Jacobson's organ**
(JAY-kub-sunz OR-gun) Two small sensory pits in the roof of the mouth in lizards and snakes. The organ analyzes molecules picked up from the air or ground and carried to the organ by the tongue.

**keratin** (KER-uh-tun) A material found in horns and fingernails.

**plastron** (PLAS-tron) The bottom part of a turtle's or tortoise's shell.

**predator** (PREH-duh-ter) An animal that hunts and eats other animals.

**scales** (SKAYLZ) Distinct, thick areas of a reptile's skin.

**scutes** (SKOOTS) The horny plates that cover a turtle's or tortoise's bony shell.

**throat flap**
(THROHT FLAP) A valve at the back of a crocodilian's throat that closes to stop water from entering the windpipe when the animal is eating prey underwater.

**venomous**
(VEH-nuh-mis) Poisonous; able to immobilize or kill prey or predators.

**vertebrates**
(VER-tih-brits) Animals that have backbones.

# Index

# Websites

Due to the changing nature of Internet links, PowerKids Press has developed an online list of websites related to the subject of this book. This site is updated regularly. Please use this link to access the list:

www.powerkidslinks.com/disc/rept/